When Times Are Tough

Marie Murray is a clinical psychologist and *Irish Times* columnist, author and broadcaster. She has been a weekly radio contributor to *Today with Pat Kenny* (2000–2003), the transcripts of which, together with a selection of her *Irish Times* columns, were published in a collection entitled *Living Our Times* in 2007. Other radio series and books have included *Nervous Breakdown* (1994), *The Stress Files* (1997), *On Your Marks* (1999) and *Surviving The Leaving Cert* (2002). Selections from her *Time-Out Irish Times* column and *Mindtime*, her weekly psychology series on RTÉ Radio One's *Drivetime with Mary Wilson*, are reproduced in this volume. She is a Registered Psychologist, Registered Family Therapist and Supervisor, and a Registered Member of the European Association for Psychotherapy.

WHEN TIMES
ARE TOUGH

Marie Murray

A collection of her columns from The Irish Times

VERITAS

Published 2011 by
Veritas Publications
7–8 Lower Abbey Street
Dublin 1, Ireland
publications@veritas.ie
www.veritas.ie

ISBN 978 1 84730 262 5
Copyright © Marie Murray, 2011

The articles published herein first appeared in and are reproduced by
kind permission of *The Irish Times*.

10 9 8 7 6 5 4 3 2 1

A catalogue record for this book is available from the British Library.

Designed by Tanya M. Ross, Veritas
Printed in the Republic of Ireland by Hudson Killeen, Dublin

Veritas books are printed on paper made from the wood pulp of managed
forests. For every tree felled, at least one tree is planted, thereby renewing
natural resources.

When Times Are Tough confronts the tough economic times in which we live with understanding, humour, clinical compassion, common-sense and a wealth of imaginative ideas on how to make life rich in recessionary times. It offers a reminder that even in the midst of uncertainty and upheaval, there are always things to celebrate and savour. It points to the possibility and potential in the simplest of everyday things and offers encouragement for the times when the sparkle dims and energy fails. It recognises the strength of the human spirit, the wealth in relationships and the value of solidarity, conveyed even in something as simple as a hug.

With a lightness of touch and a depth of insight, its pages hold something of value for everyone at all stages of life. It is a book to keep nearby to dip into any time a cheerful note, practical advice, sound psychological sense or a reassuring voice is required. Drawing together a selection of the author's *Irish Times* Health Columns and topics from her RTÉ radio *Drivetime* slot, the book responds to the questions and quandaries of life in an astute and affirming way.

THIS BOOK IS DEDICATED TO ALL THOSE FOR WHOM THESE TIMES
IN WHICH WE LIVE ARE TOUGH.

Contents

In Praise of the Champagne Flute

There are a number of symbols of fine living, of indulgence, of extravagance, even of decadence. Principal amongst these must be the champagne flute. Its crafted curvature, its delicate stem, its sensuous lip and its elongated elegance are unique. The flute is a work of art. It is lovely to hold, a delight to behold, and it contains an elixir, the name alone of which ignites a sense of occasion, of celebration and of joy.

There is no ambivalence about a glass of champagne. When the flute appears, good things are happening and they are to be noted and toasted with a drink and a clink and an appreciation of life.

The flute has one purpose only. It accommodates only one potion. It is shaped for that purpose and none other. It cannot facilitate a glass of milk, would make nonsense of the froth on a pint, would destroy a brandy and intimidate a beer. It would confound the temperature of wine and would be insulted by a soda. It would refuse a sherry, and while it might collude with a cocktail to have it delivered to its own elegant glass, it must secretly disdain the uncouth accoutrements that bedeck that beverage. The flute is understated. That is its strength.

The flute will not join glassware in a dishwasher. It will not occupy a cramped cupboard. It will not jostle for room. It stands alone, elegantly and eloquently proclaiming its special status in its unique space.

The flute knows its place and places itself at the centre of celebration. It is not intended to be utilitarian and would reject such functionality. It is not designed for the downing of alcohol, but for raising the tone of life, and it knows it.

The flute is not greedy. It merely requires that it be half-filled. Excess is anathema to its sensibility. It does not want loud popping of corks or excessive bubbles. It does not contain a drink to be guzzled. The delicacy of its frame discourages that. It does not condone overindulgence. Its contents are to be savoured. Its temperature is to be regulated. Its use judicious but joyful. Its secret lies in the capacity of a little to inebriate.

The flute's power is psychological as much as physiological. It is symbolic. That is what makes the bringing forth of flutes portentous. There is palaver about it, but it does not disappoint. The flute may be paraded but there is purpose in doing so, whether one is congratulating, or sharing, consoling or celebrating, with family or friends. It says we are together. It says we will mark this time. It says that just for now all the ordinary in life is suspended and what is enjoyable is to be entertained. Without the flute, champagne would be insignificant. Its taste would be destroyed in a tumbler. The flute is part of the felicity.

It would be wrong to think that the flute is inappropriate in times of recession. While it may be made of finest iridescent crystal, it can equally be fashioned of sterner stuff without sacrificing the essence of its shape and itself. Nor does it require frequent use or even extravagant replenishment when it is used. That is its advantage.

The flute can wait. It charges nothing for waiting but encourages by its presence. That presence is a promise. The flute can be unfilled without its purpose being unfulfilled. It is a reminder of past happiness and future potential. No matter how bleak the time may be, it knows that it will be required again, some time, some day for some celebration for someone.

And champagne is not prohibited in times of sadness either. Lady Bollinger, of the Bollinger brand of champagnes, famously said that she drank champagne when happy and when sad, found it comforting when she was alone and obligatory when she had company, trifled with it when she was not hungry and drank it when she was, but otherwise never drank champagne except when thirsty!

Such use of the flute is not to be recommended, but a little of what you fancy is always good for the psyche. The occasional Magnum on a celebratory occasion lifts the spirits and probably costs no more than a few rounds of less festive drinks. We need to learn how to 'do without' in these difficult times, but also, if we are fortunate enough, to still have enough, to be glad that we have what we have, and to do what we do with humour, *joie de vivre* and a spirit of exuberance. Sometimes, that may be done by raising a flute to the future.

Biding Time When Times Are Tough

Biding time is a specific concept of time allocation. It is different to spending time, which has a commercial ring to it. It differs from saving time, which equally implies some financial investment. Biding time is about patience. It is about letting life unfold in its own time. It is not about hurrying towards a specific goal but knowing that change can come about equally well by waiting. Biding time lets what needs to be revealed, reveal itself, and emerge in its own time, unhurried by human interference.

Biding time is similar to but not the same as waiting. Waiting is a goal-oriented, active process. We wait for something that is specific and that we have expectations of arriving, or occurring, in a measurable period of time.

Biding time has a gentler pace. It allows time to pass by in its own way, knowing that what will be, will be. It is about having patience and understanding that what is destined to happen will occur in its own time without human intervention.

Our relationship with time has a deep psychology. It is complex. It is ambivalent. It changes with the passage of time itself. Time is not just something that we measure, allocate, determine and expend. While we have command over how we use it, it always has the greater power. While we may wait for time to pass and for anticipated events to arrive, time does not wait for us.

Time progresses regardless of our wishes, interventions or attempts to arrest it. We are both beneficiaries of its bounty and at its absolute mercy. Time does not pause when we would wish it to, nor will it advance speedily from that which we wish to avoid; it will not hurry towards what we desire or return to what we might wish to revisit. It has its own pace concurrent with our lives and how we live them, irrespective of how we do so.

Our existence is measured by time from birth to death and these dates are marked on our last resting place. We are each allocated a quota.

How we spend it is up to us. Whether we enjoy it, savour it, apportion it, share it with others, assign it to specific activities, plan our use of it or see what it brings depends upon us, our construal of time and our personal motivations.

Or so we think.

Our relationship with time is not just personally significant, it has other implications depending upon how it is construed and used in families, in social groups, nationally and internationally.

This is why when we mess with time we hurt the present and damage the future in a way that has serious consequences for everyone in society. For example, we have been through one of the least admirable economic phases in our country's history, essentially based on the maxim 'time is money'. Time became a fiscal measure rather than a human one. Investment in property and shares rather than people dominated thinking. Time's relevance was economically determined, time's passage financially evaluated and the future determined in terms of asset appreciation with time.

Now we wait for time to recompense the errors of such thinking, for time to recoup our losses, return us to fiscal security and bring future compensation if we 'share the pain' and exert prudence in the present.

But those being asked to bide their time, to defer their pensions, to give time to solve what others created are angry: not about the loss of money, but about the loss of time. For many this is time they can ill afford to spend on enjoying what was promised, reap what they worked towards, benefit by what they saved for, what they invested in, what they believed they would have and deserved, having served their time in thriftiness. They cannot bide their time.

It takes time to get the measure of time, to appreciate its limits and to learn how to resource it. With the passage of time comes understanding that time is the most valuable currency one can possess and the theft of time a most abusive theft. This is why there is such anger towards those who tainted time with money in unholy profligate alliances, through which the most valuable asset of time has been stolen from everyone.

Nurturing the Sole

The therapeutic activity of washing feet is greatly overlooked. This is unfortunate, because foot-washing is a simple remedial intervention requiring no more than a bidet or a basin of comfortably hot water and whatever emollients one prefers to use to soothe the feet.

Washing feet is an extraordinarily effective way to de-stress, not least because it is simple, available, can be undertaken swiftly in situations of necessity, or can provide whole hours of self-indulgence that ensure a return to emotional equilibrium.

The restorative nature of foot-washing lies in the combination of activities involved. Firstly there is the decision to foot-wash. This acknowledges that relaxation is needed and that a ritual as ancient as time itself is to be undertaken to do so. Secondly, getting the temperature of the water right is imperative. This is a delicate testing operation that displaces other concerns, because there is nothing as uncomfortable as putting one's foot into water that is either too hot or too cold. Water for foot-washing has to be just right. Thirdly, the moment when sore feet are submerged in warm water is a moment of physical ecstasy and psychological release, providing a time to consciously imagine releasing all the worries of the day out through the feet.

While washing feet can take place anywhere in the house, veteran foot-washers understand the consideration this decision demands. For some, a dedicated space with all the accoutrements ready for ablution guarantees that they attend to their feet every single day. Some people like to take a prominent position in front of the television and enjoy the triple pleasure of solitude, foot-washing and entertainment, because washing feet is the fastest way to clear a room of occupants. Corns and calluses and other people's bunions are not a pretty sight.

Some people make a ritual of foot-washing, with low lights, scented candles, fluffy towels to enfold the feet and rich, thick moisturising creams to complete the rite. Some people are pragmatic: washing their feet after running, dancing or sport activities or perfunctorily at the end of each day.

For others, daily dousing is part of their health regime, central to good physical and mental well-being; they know that foot-washing is not to be undertaken lightly but to be engaged in with due seriousness and intent. The treatment of diabetes stresses that feet be kept healthy and that any cuts, abrasions, or ulcers are treated immediately. Foot massage is recommended for stress. Lavender foot-soaks assist sleep, and anyone who remembers the hot water bottle will recall the regressive reassurance of a hot bottle on icy feet in a cold bed.

When you wash your feet you wash your life. You become aware of the expenditure of your physical and emotional energy. You are conscious if you have been 'on your feet' all day – the toll that can take on your well-being, and the importance of 'putting your feet up', of taking time out for yourself for a while every day. Foot-washing is more than washing the feet. It is an art ancient and new across eastern and western cultures. Washing the feet of another has signified hospitality, reverence, communion and community since time began. The washing of feet features in many religious faiths, ordinances and observances and is a practice both simple and profound, of honour, servitude, submission and celebration. Since biblical times there have been potent examples of feet-washing as acts of love, of humility, of piety, of respect, of equality, of contrition, of courtesy and of care.

Feet are metaphorical and emotional barometers. To get 'cold feet' is to lose confidence in oneself; to 'put one's foot in it' is to make a mistake; to have 'two left feet' is to feel awkward and clumsy; while 'putting the best foot forward' is a statement of courage and intent.

Feet are diagnostic. Before there were weather forecasts, there were men and women's feet to foretell if rain was on the way. When our great-grandmothers sat and soaked their feet, pared their corns and predicted rain based on how itchy and inflamed those poor corns were, they never imagined that they were doing something as highfaluting as chiropody or as elite as psychosomatic care.

But even before podiatry, people knew that if you didn't take care of your feet, you'd have pains in your back. Before there were foot spas, there were basins of soapy water. Before reflexology, people implicitly understood that if their feet were 'killing them', their general health needed attention. They knew that kneading the foot was good for the sole.

On Times Past: The Psychology of Frugality

Frugality is the practice of self-restraint, self-denial, of thrift, prudence and economy in consumption. Recently it has been rediscovered, revisited and revised. Necessity has always been a great re-inventor of old inventions. And so frugality is being updated and upgraded for a generation that never heard about it before, or who perhaps regarded it as miserliness, as tight-fisted, penny-pinching mealy-minded stinginess.

It is extraordinary to witness frugality emerging as a new, exciting, environmentally friendly, ecologically sound, behaviourally restrained economic concept and practice. Yet to a generation that remembers the middle of the last century, frugality was a way of life enshrined in thinking and practice as if it were constitutional.

Solid, hardworking, modest living was respected: 'the honest crust' and the work that produced 'the daily bread'. There was virtue in 'making do', which was an art form of creativity, of lateral thinking and which, in hindsight, demonstrated a natural intelligence illusive to psychological measurement on academic or psychometric scales, but powerful and productive in its time.

That is why the new high status that the concept of frugality is enjoying is amusing to the generation that practiced it decades ago, many of whom most wisely never discontinued the practice, despite all societal inducements to do so. This is because they knew, instinctively, the simple maxim that 'what goes up must come down', and that includes inflation.

Many of us grew up in an era that recycled before the word was invented; an era when 'waste not want not' was respected; when every object had at least a second use; when the brown paper wrapping on the 'parcel from America' was folded and saved to cover school books, the string stored, the stamps collected for the 'missions', and the contents of that box of shiny objects and colourful clothes relished for their

garish gaiety and outrageous luxury. They were symbols of unimaginable consumerism from the other side of the Atlantic, consumption that was alien, at the time, to these shores.

Those who remember the former incarnation of frugality will confirm that it was more than thriftiness, more than carefulness, more than cost-consciousness, sparing, saving, parsimonious behaviour. It was more than prudent management of limited resources. It was ingrained. It was ideological. It was ethical practice. It was a moral imperative. Its converse was a 'sin'. The parable of 'the talents' was known, whereby one had a duty to use one's gifts wisely and to share them with others generously.

Frugality was practiced as a household norm. Who of that time will not remember the ordinary, everyday frugality: the darning and mending, the hand-me-downs from eldest to youngest, the hems turned up and down, the buttons replaced, shoes heeled, mended and polished to perfection on Saturday nights.

Wardrobes were small, possessions were few. Quality, not quantity, was what counted. Clothes were bought big and grown into. There was 'the good coat', the 'Sunday best' and the 'everyday'. The burden of decision about what to wear was not upon child or adult because choices were few.

It was a generation that did not encourage too much 'dressing up' or 'showing off'. Wealth, if one was fortunate to be blessed with it, was understated, inconspicuous and discreet. Leftovers became shepherd's pie. Home produce, to which we are now returning, was the order of the day. A society that atavistically remembered the Famine did not waste anything edible at all.

This is not to idealise a time that had its own most serious difficulties, to pretend that terrible poverty did not exist, or to deny a different kind of gloom, pessimism, darkness, dreariness and dread that hung over a people in a new Republic struggling to find an identity. But if research has shown the psychological benefits of the practice of frugality versus a materialistic ethos, then re-appropriating frugality is worthwhile.

Materialism has been linked psychologically with less well-being, problematic relationships, more competitive and less cooperative behaviour, with more ecologically degrading behaviour, higher carbon footprints and less generosity.

Frugality as a chosen practice has been equated with greater happiness, self-esteem, self-control, lower anxiety and with greater generosity and altruism. Imagine: we practiced it before psychology measured it.

Less is more!

—5—

Fine, Just Fine

How are you'? ...'I'm fine.' So common, so predictable, so nebulous, yet so conventional is the response 'I'm fine' to the formulaic 'How are you?' that it has applicability in every affective instance one could imagine. Regardless of mood, disposition, state of health, mental turmoil or quiescence, in the midst of tragedy, or at the summit of happiness, in all of these instances it is not inappropriate to answer 'I'm fine' when asked how we are.

'I'm fine' has the capacity to mean anything, to mean everything and to mean nothing at all. It is a wonderful utterance. It can be voiced with a chirpy assurance, a dolorous exhalation, a bland neutrality, a humorous evasion, a stoical reassurance or with the most wonderful, guilt-inducing sigh. 'Don't mind me – you go out and enjoy yourself. I'm fine.'

'I'm fine' is endlessly creative. It means whatever you wish it to mean, whatever you wish the recipient to interpret. Now what other utterance in the English language does that? It always succeeds. Its simplicity is stunning. Its brevity is powerful. Its convenience is invaluable. Its semiotics are impenetrable. That is why we love it, that is why we use it and that is why we retain it in social exchange.

Of course how one responds to 'I'm fine' and the nuances with which it is uttered depend upon the relationship between questioner and respondent. The sharp, definitive, clipped 'I'm fine' invites no further commentary and no additional interrogation. It can mean that the state of the respondent is no business of the interviewer. It can mean that the subject is not for discussion. Or it can mean that this is not the appropriate moment to disclose one's feelings.

Equally, the initial 'How are you?' may open or close conversations. It may be asked by stopping for an answer or by passing by swiftly. It may be perfunctory, casual or a most genuine wish to understand how another person feels.

Asking someone how they are does not necessarily lack solicitude. Context determines meaning. For example, the parameters of 'How

are you?', 'I'm fine' are usually understood as ambulant greetings in the workplace, where in the busyness of the day they convey hello and goodbye simultaneously, while also saying I see you, I recognise you, and if time permitted we might engage in conversation.

Social convention demands that we know the circumstances in which to ask and answer questions, the boundaries around them, the relational contexts in which we omit, restrict or extend them and the levels of information we provide in response to them, all depending upon who is asking the question and the situation in which the question is being asked.

But it is in marital relationships that 'I'm fine' comes into its own. 'I'm fine' in marital exchange can be deeply nuanced if provided by a woman in the aftermath of a difference in views! Men fear it most because 'I'm fine' is often so semantically laden that most men know they will fail to decode it precisely: the deep structures of intersubjective affective communication being something at which they are traditionally less skilled and less practiced in deciphering.

A man knows that if another man says he is fine, that he should accept that response. Face value is valued amongst men. But men equally know that this does not usually apply when a woman says, 'I'm fine'. Men know that women's semantic dexterity will outwit them every time: that 'fine' may not mean fine; that 'fine' may mean a whole range of things that he has to understand quickly; that 'fine' may signal an offence which he must interpret and respond to with alacrity, sensitivity, contrition and the correct answer. This is a feat that defeats the majority of men.

In the discussion between John Bridger and Charlie Croker before the robbery in the film *The Italian Job*, they agree that 'I'm fine' really means 'freaked out, insecure, neurotic and emotional'. They seem to recognise that men hide their anxiety from each other behind the stock assurance that they are fine and that men don't expect each other to investigate it further. What is most interesting about their conversation is that instead of saying how they feel, they agree that not saying how they feel curiously reveals how they feel, and in this paradoxical way they manage to articulate their actual feelings to each other.

Now if you can follow that, you are probably a woman, and if not, you are a man, and that's fine!

Radio − The Perfect Relationship

Is there anything more intimate than the radio? The marvel of Marconi never wears. It speaks to us when we desire company and is silent when peace is our want. It is by turn informative, instructive, inspirational, entertaining, engaging and enraging, trivial and profound, calming and energising − a backdrop to our lives.

The radio is company when we are alone. It is companionable when we walk. It is a passenger in our cars. It is patient in our pockets. It whispers secretly to us on Dart, Luas, bus or train. It protects us from external chatter. When we are ill it is beside us. When we are sad it distracts us. When we are happy it complements our mood.

Like the village gossip, the radio knows what is happening and tells all. Each day it scuttles and scurries with every titbit of news, recording and repeating the latest events, what people think about them, who is saying what, going where, doing what, with whom, when and why.

Was there ever a gossip so efficient? Yet unlike the gossip, the radio allows us to listen impartially and it does not pry for reciprocal, salacious reward for its hearsay. It begins our day. It bids us goodnight.

The radio makes no demands. It does not stipulate that we be attentive to its voice, that we sit and listen to its conversation, that we agree with what it has to say, that we respond to its message, that we deliberate on its proposals, concur with its propositions or defend its arguments. It allows us to eavesdrop and earwig blatantly and brazenly on everything it says.

The radio is the perfect companion. It is not offended if we work while in its company. It allows us to tune in and out of its discussions. It is narcissistic in its ceaseless chatter but without ego in requiring no response.

Nor does it demand eye contact to reassure it that we are attentive. It makes no protest when we silence it and it responds immediately when we call upon its company again. It is available, accessible, responsive,

reliable, loyal, steadfast and present at our command. It costs little and enriches our lives.

Radio has a distinct advantage over visual media. What we see on radio we see with the mind's eye. Radio respects our imagination, recognises our capacity to visualise what we hear, to colour what we envision and see with our own minds. Like the sensory cross-activation of synaesthesia – that wonderful confusion of senses where one sense triggers another – radio allows us to hear colour, see sound, taste music, feel conversation. It is indeed a rich inter-sensorial world.

Unlike the busyness of television, the hyperactivity of internet, the insistence of mobile phone, the publicity of Twitter and the rigidity of print, radio is personal in its communication. There is primordial reassurance in listening to the human voice, a regressive intrauterine experience of voice murmur, intimate yet distant in an audio bubble of existence that is at once familiar and strange, personal, impersonal and ever-present. There is reassurance in listening to the sounds of one's own language, the strains of one's culture, the dialect of one's tradition and the reassurance of its tone.

Before Ireland was plural, multicultural, cosmopolitan, global, it was magic to access, with the turn of a dial, the incomprehensibility of other tongues, the sense of other places and music that was unfamiliar to our ears.

We have memories of radio, stored memories of a lyric, a snatch of music, a news intro, a programme intro, a media voice, a seminal event that we heard about on radio or an ordinary event in our own lives that radio accompanied. It takes but the crackle of airwave to recall those events and re-experience all the emotions that accompanied them.

There is a wonderful moment in Frank McGuinness' screenplay of Brian Friel's drama *Dancing at Lughnasa* when the radio in the house kicks into life and the sisters one by one are seduced into dance by the traditional jig playing. They abandon all that oppresses them and disregard all that restrains them in unruly ritualistic confluence of time and place, music and tradition, past and present, all that was longed for but never achieved and all that was achieved at the expense of their happiness.

For those moments brought to them by radio, they ignite and recognise the dormant passions of their parched lives and the loves that might be possible for them, in a wild abandon that unites them in their shared history, separateness and togetherness. And that is radio.

Forget sociological analysis or psychological investigation: the radio is present, personal and persistent, and while technologies may advance, I challenge any to overtake this intimate stranger with whom we share our lives.

−7−

Our Reflections

Mirrors are magic. They mesmerise. They illuminate. They reflect our physical being and psychological presence. They provide our first visual encounter with ourselves. They may even determine when existence has ended – when no breath exhales to shadow the surface of a mirror held to the face.

We do well to reflect upon mirrors. They are objects of psychological significance in our lives.

When the Venetians perfected the art of mirror making, they revealed previously inaccessible worlds: spiritual, scientific, optical and conceptual worlds, distant worlds through the telescope; metaphors for writers and self-portraiture for artists. The mirror is a source of poetic imagination, philosophical investigation, psychological speculation and artistic inspiration summed up best, perhaps, in Dutch artist M.C. Escher's *Hand with Reflecting Sphere*.

Mirrors advance the development of identity and individuality and the integration of external and interior selves. As psychoanalytic adherents of the Lacanian 'mirror-stage' in infancy explain, the 'jubilation' when a child first recognises its mirror-image heralds not only understanding of itself as a unified self, but also as separate and individuated from others. This sight of self is an important developmental milestone.

Mirrors magically accommodate imperceptible visual alterations in our appearance from day to day and the sameness and difference of our person over decades. We hold in our memories the imprints of a lifetime of looking at ourselves: a paradoxical narcissism and insecurity and visual archive of our existence.

Mirrors may be our harshest critics and most vain admirers. Sylvia Plath described the mirror as 'not cruel, only truthful', yet Pablo Picasso's *Girl Before a Mirror* represents the fragmentation of self in reflection, reminding us of the disjunction there may be between outer and inner experiences of self.

Mirrors reflect us only as accurately or inexactly as we are willing to see. In this the mirror is both truth and illusion. It may turn our 'inner worthiness into the eye' or distort what we contort. It may record what has befallen us or fail to portray the extent of sorrow etched upon our souls. Shakespeare's Richard II, looking into his 'glass', wonders how sorrow could have struck so many blows upon his face and 'made no deeper wounds', before he shatters the mirror, thus symbolising his broken self.

A potent illustration of anorexia nervosa is the person with the emaciated body looking into the mirror and seeing an obese figure. The delusional dysmorphophobic belief of having a deformity by those who objectively have no facial or bodily abnormalities, sends sufferers to endless mirror checking, total avoidance of mirrors, or quests for excessive, unnecessary cosmetic surgery. We need to look beyond the surface of self into a self that resides within and know its worth.

Mirrors may also intentionally deceive. The smoke and mirror illusions of conjurers or the concave mirrors of carnivals provide cartoon likenesses of ourselves with weirdly enlarged or elongated bodies or diminutive or contorted figures that dismantle vanity, feed flights of fancy and validate the possibility of parallel worlds 'through the looking glass'.

Nor is it surprising that many superstitions surround mirrors, not least the seven years' bad luck consequent upon breaking one unless the fragments are buried by moonlight. The Irish tradition of covering mirrors when a person died ensured that the soul would not take fright or lose its way when making its exit from the world. Vampires have traditionally been identified by the lack of a reflection in mirrors, and looking into a mirror whilst holding a lighted candle is meant to reveal more than we might want from 'the other side'. All of these myths must contribute to the phobic fear of mirrors, or eisoptrophobia.

There is a strange symbiosis between person and object. The mirror is but a shiny surface without our gaze, while we are blind to ourselves without its reciprocal stare. We inhabit it when we look into it. To paraphrase another Shakespearean figure, Julius Caesar, since we cannot see ourselves 'so well as by reflection', mirrors discover to ourselves that of ourselves which we yet know not of.

When we scrutinise ourselves in a mirror, read its reflections, examine our emotions, dare to look deep into our own eyes, visually trace each outline in the face, follow its contours, discover our distinctiveness, focus on our individuality and accept our reality, then we encounter ourselves, the shards of our existence and the totality of our selves.

Time Out

Time out is time well spent. It is taking time out of the day for oneself, commandeering time for personal use and benefit. It is time away from tasks. The purpose of time out is to do something exclusively for ourselves that brings light into our day.

Time out is a reprieve from drudgery. It connects us to what matters to us, what enlivens, engages and enriches us. It is special. It is not given. It must be taken. We talk of 'taking' time out because it is precious time that we must requisition or else it is lost. Time out is a gift we bestow on ourselves by factoring it into each day, each week, into our lives. We take time out when we do something that we love every day.

If we can have moments that rejuvenate us, read something that inspires us, hear something that moves us, see something that stirs our emotions, think of something that soothes us, smell something that reassures us, do something that invigorates us, then we are truly taking time out.

Taking time out is a habit to be encouraged. It does not require large swathes of time. Sometimes minutes suffice. But it is lost if we do not claim it. That is why time out must be seized, without guilt, on a regular basis, to maintain personal happiness and health. We can withstand much if we give ourselves at least a little time out for ourselves each day.

This is one of the more interesting facets of the research in relation to stress: the degree to which we can cope with considerable strain if we simply ensure some recuperative time during it. For example, Hans Selye, one of the fathers of stress theory, demonstrated in his 'general adaptation syndrome' the stress stages through which we progress, from alarm to exhaustion, if we do not have a restorative reprieve in the process.

There are psychological consequences if we do not take time out, such as problems in concentration, in memory, in energy, in sleep, in self-esteem and in mood. There may be work-related problems, in efficiency, with illness or absenteeism and occupational burn-out if we do not extricate ourselves from demands for at least a short time each day.

Our resistance to stress is remarkably good if we take time out for ourselves. And as stress increases in the workplace, or in job seeking, in financial concerns, in relationships, in family pressures and in the pessimistic milieu of recent times, we need to resource ourselves much more than we do.

The annual holiday does not do it. The short break, while valuable, cannot replace it. Time out: taking personal, reflective or sociable, enjoyable space each day promotes psychological resilience.

Time out is not just time off. It has a deeper meaning. It is often about ensuring solitude. Frequently a much-loved piece of music is all that is required. For some a short walk provides it. For others vigorous exercise. Some people imagine or remember a particular physical place. Many take time out by becoming conscious of their breathing, their bodies, by systematically releasing tension from muscles, tuning out the world and tuning in to themselves.

Some find their daily solace in religious exercise. A surprising number of people 'stop and stare'. They take a specific object and reflect on it – its outline, its colour, texture and quality. Like still-life artists, they attune to the detail of inanimate objects or living things.

Of course hermits, contemplatives, recluses and those who crave solitude may spend their entire lives away from the fray. Many writers, artists, poets and others find that they need to sequester themselves from excessive interaction with others to access their creativity. But all of us need to make and take short scraps of time out for ourselves.

One efficacious time-out strategy is what might be called mental mooching. This allows the mind to drift, without purpose, intent, task, goal or required outcome, and engage in just thinking thoughts about things. Mental mooching is cogitation. This cogitation – wonderful, ruminative, meditative pondering – may be about something, or about nothing, about living, or life itself, mulling over who we are, what we are, how we got here and where we are going.

Sure didn't Descartes, the ultimate cogitator, take serious time out to decide that his thinking confirmed his existence. And think what happened for Newton when he took time out to sit under a tree. Archimedes showed the value of time out having a bath. There is no doubt about it: time out is time well spent.

—9—

A Nice Cup of Tea

Would you like a nice cup of tea? The question raises the curiosity of those unfamiliar with our language and the vast and particular vocabulary that surrounds our discussions about tea. We have been offering each other 'a nice cup of tea' for so long that we have never considered the antonymous alternative to that offer. Besides, nobody in Ireland could ever make a nasty cup of tea. We are too long making it, living on it, loving it, offering it, drinking it, requesting it, refusing it and socially interacting because of it, that we all know how to make a nice cup of tea.

Our offers of tea extend well beyond 'nice' to many different kinds of tea, including 'a little' cup of tea. This diminutive descriptor takes the harm out of our generosity so that guests won't feel obligated when it is only a 'little' cup.

Tea is always available. Sure 'the kettle is already boiled', or 'it will only take a minute to boil' or 'it will be ready in no time', and if anyone says they are in a hurry there is always the offer of 'a cup in your hand' or 'a quick cup of tea'. When all else fails in our offers of tea, the assiduity of Mrs Doyle is required with 'ah go on, go on, go on' until capitulation.

There is a hereditary Irish impulse to ensure that if we are not imbibing alcohol we are at least consuming tea. And while we may not always want the tea we are required to drink, not to be offered a cup of tea is a serious social gaffe bringing forth that wonderful phrase, 'Did they think I hadn't a mouth on me?' Because next to talking, tea drinking is one of our fine Irish talents, and an Irish mouth not engaged in one or other activity is a deviance indeed.

We love a 'drop' of tea, and when guests are halfway into their nice cup of tea we ask if they would like a 'hot drop', extending the teapot and ensuring that an entire cup is never entirely consumed without at least one top-up. Thereafter it becomes necessary to have a 'fresh pot' because no conversation was ever completed over just one pot of tea.

Childhood indoctrination into the world of tea commences with the 'lullaby of boiling kettle' and perfecting the song and gestures of 'I'm a

little teapot' and 'Polly put the kettle on'. This early identity confusion may account for later addiction, for few of us could get through a day without tea's infusion. 'Teatotallers' are sparse in Irish society and 'The Emergency' is remembered for the rationing of tea and of sugar with which to douse it.

Early conditioning to 'the leaf that gives its spell' may also account for the attachment of workmen to tea, while research on the frequency, intensity and duration of 'tea breaks' indicate that they exceed working time. Perhaps reform in public services and private enterprise might also be achieved by prohibition, were it not for the consequent psychological ill-health that would ensue.

So integral is tea to our psychological well-being that all calamities require the kettle and we are blithe in disregard of caveats on caffeine, tannin, theine and theanine. For what are they, we say, compared to the cup that comforts in times of need? We administer tea to ourselves and bestow it on others, and if no sage advice is forthcoming for someone in distress there is a cuppa to proffer: that, in itself, is a therapeutic act.

Tea is ease and elixir. As Lu Yu, the Sage of Tea, had it: 'Tea tempers the spirit and harmonises the mind.' Sugared it soothes us in shock. At morn it wakes us, at elevenses it enlivens us, it punctuates the afternoon, accompanies high tea, is a must at suppertime and at all other intervals when one is parched or partial to a good cup of tea.

And in our going it accompanies us, for there was never a 'wake' at which tea did not flow with the anecdotes and celebrations of the life of the dead. Yes, tea to us Irish is more than a beverage.

In this time of recession when we despair of the past and fear for the future and when the pot is empty and we have consumed all that we could absorb, we can look into our empty cups that once overflowed and read in the leaves portents of what lies ahead.

Disappointment

We tend to regard emotions as feelings that are powerful, passionate, surging and strong. 'Disappointment' is a quieter emotion, even though it may be intensely felt. It is the failure of expectations, a feeling of being let down by oneself or by others, by circumstances, or by unfortunate or unexpected events. It is related to disillusionment because trust is discredited and beliefs have to be revised.

Disappointment is different to regret, although there may be a wish to have made alternative decisions in life or a belief that by doing so life might have been different and less disappointing. It is different because while we may, of course, be disappointed in ourselves, disappointment often comes about through the action or inaction of others. Regret tends to be more personal and internal and to relate more to things that were in our control.

While the origin of the emotions of disappointment and regret may differ, the feelings are often remarkably the same. They are visceral, bodily, physically felt. They include a heaviness, a sadness, a sense of loss, of let-down, of weight and of defeat.

Disappointment is felt when what we had expected to happen does not happen, when anticipated responses or rewards do not materialise. It is not achieving what one had expected to achieve, not receiving what one had expected to receive, not attaining what one had expected to attain. It is when a belief has to be altered, a hope abandoned, an expectation foregone and a sense of loss accommodated.

Disappointment can relate to job loss, job change, promotion and career development, life opportunities, sports, finances, family dynamics, friendships and personal relationships. Situations that disappoint can range from trivial to significant, and the intensity and duration of the feelings of disappointment will depend on that.

Disappointment is an experience that one may have at any time and during any life stage. Few lives, if any, are lived without their human share of disappointments. While there are objective disappointments,

the subjective appraisal of them also plays a part, influencing whether or not they taint subsequent experiences in life.

Psychological theory shows that disappointment-avoidant cultures are problematic because they suggest entitlement to perfection and practice unhealthy avoidance of normal upset. They do not encourage acceptance and natural resilience when things go wrong, even though these are skills that are needed from childhood throughout life. Tough times are inevitable at some stage in life. Knowing how to deal with these times realistically, while also maintaining hopefulness that things can change for the better as suddenly as they changed for the worse, is important psychologically. We all need this skill.

Childhood disappointments may be transitory but they have special intensity. The first disappointment a child encounters initiates the child into the experience of disappointment itself. Disappointment in childhood can involve the toppling of parental gods, the revelation that the world is not perfect, nor the people in it, the realisation that promises can be broken, that magic is not available and that all wishes do not come true.

Disappointment in adolescence is often centred on the self, on identity, on appearance, on acceptance and on attainment *vis-à-vis* peers. It can arise out of expectation shaped by society that is impossible to meet. It can arise through pressure to be of a certain size, attitude, personality, style – dictated by market forces and unrealistic norms. It can come from a deep longing to belong and distress at not knowing how to achieve this.

Disappointment is a complex emotion and an intense one. It is often sorted simply by time: time which makes what seems crucial today irrelevant tomorrow, time which reveals who are true friends and who are temporary, time which shows what is important and what is not, and time which allows the unfolding of what people are meant to be if they can trust in it.

Young people come to understand that there are gradations of emotions in life: of happiness and sadness; contentment and dissatisfaction; loss and gain; intimacy and detachment; acceptance and rejection; triumph and defeat. This too takes time to appreciate.

Of course disappointments in middle and later life are often felt acutely, because there is the sense of less time being available to redress them. Major disappointments are distressing when people cannot go back and start again: to parent differently; make wiser financial decisions; use their time more happily with family; invest more in friendships; or take alternative career paths.

As people reflect on their lives, they often realise how much they know now that they wish they had understood earlier. They can be disappointed about potential that was not fulfilled; goals not achieved; talent not supported; ability not encouraged; possibilities not brought to fruition; risks not taken. It can seem too late to catch up on dreams.

Just as in childhood there is added potency to disappointment because of what it conveys about the future, in later life there is added poignancy to disappointment when people look back on the past and on things they wish they could rectify, alter or resolve. They think it is too late for change. But that is rarely so. The past is not such a foreign country that it cannot be revisited, and the future is an even more exciting, unexplored terrain. New dreams can always be made. It would be a mistake to think it is ever too late to redress disappointments. Negative beliefs close off options. We deal with disappointment by accepting the normal vicissitudes of life, by task analysis and setting concrete steps towards realistic goals, by planning ahead, by finding role models for what we want to accomplish, by optimism and by abandoning inappropriate frustration, disillusionment, guilt and blame about decisions that we made in the past. Whatever about disappointments of the past, let's not make future ones when so much psychological research confirms our capacity to alter our world significantly when we remain positive and decide to do so.

– 11 –

Where Does It Hurt?

Pain is protective. It is the body's alarm system. It is functional. It is crucial for survival. It is excruciatingly effective. It signals indisputably that something physiological is awry that requires immediate attention. It is our most important diagnostic tool. It is the means by which the site, the cause and the solution to illness may be identified. Where does it hurt? Pain tells us.

Pain is at its most proficient when it causes reflexive withdrawal from a dangerous source: fire and sharp implements for example. The acute pain from imminent danger is defensive if aversive. The throbbing pain reminds us to be careful of the tender site. The dull pain demands intervention. The cessation of pain usually signals that this particular physical problem has been sorted. It is a good default system for our bodies. It works.

Pain is persistent. It continues to signal until all is well. It will not cease until the abscess is attended to, until the invasive object is removed, until the cut is healed, the eye is cleansed, the bones are mended, the stomach has settled, the throat has cleared, the neck is unlocked, or whatever ails us physically has received the required intervention to ensure safety and prolongation of our lives.

There are some acute pains that recur, unpredictably, periodically and inevitably, although precisely when they will flare up can be difficult to estimate. This makes sufferers feel vulnerable and intimidated by the potential to be ambushed by an episode at any time. Migraine is one example of episodic, acute runs of pain. Much of migraine management goes into tracing its personal patterns, learning its advanced warning signals and discovering how to achieve as much proactive defence against it as possible.

Similarly chronic pain of its nature is persistent and resistant. Like a house alarm that cannot be silenced, it disturbs long after its initial cause has been resolved and its protective function has been served. The code to dismantle it is absent to the distress of all around it.

While multiple theories abound in relation to the nature, cause, complexity and psychology of chronic pain, and while many neuropsychological

explanations add to our understanding, the reality is that pain is individual, the experience is personal, the threshold at which it arises and subsides is specific to each person, antecedents are variable and how it intrudes on individual lives is context-bound.

Biomedical models often do not extend into the inexplicable lack of isomorphism, or fit, between the site and symptoms of pain; motivational models may suggest that people seek malign or manipulative secondary gains from pain; behaviour models may imply learned behaviour rather than real experience; psychogenic models may consign the entire experience to psychological distress; while the connection between depression and pain needs more attention. For who would not be depressed when suffering the helplessness of chronic pain and who does not become physically depleted when depressed?

Depression, whether it is acute, intermittent, recurring or chronic, is real and is experienced in the body as much as in the mind. Its physical presence is often described across all the senses and many bodily manifestations. It is often described in terms of constriction, gasping for breath, as a heavy weight, dulling of senses, as shadow, immobility, shiver, chill, confusion, heaviness and terrible pounding of heart.

Pain, whatever its origin, its function and its pattern, confronts our individuality. It is subjective. It shows how hard it can be to put words on our own experiences, how deep our emotions, how little we may be understood when we need consideration, how lonely suffering is, how solitary, how personal, how difficult to describe, how much people need their accounts to be listened to, to be taken seriously, to be validated and affirmed.

Most chronic sufferers learn how time-limited compassion can be, but those who suffer extensively need continued support. Chronic pain research is clear about the extent to which depression, fear, anxiety and anger often accompany chronic pain, which alerts us to the need to intervene swiftly and systemically, exploring not just the individual's experience but the other contexts of family, friends, social relationships, belief systems and work situations where economic and organisational loss is enormous.

Where does it hurt? Life can hurt. It can do so in many ways. Unless and until we listen more to those who are hurting, whether it be physically, psychologically, occasionally, chronically or specifically, we cannot provide effective pain management. There is no thermometer: the individual who suffers is the pain barometer. Listening is the first response.

The Value of Venting

Venting is usually described as the release of emotion in an outburst. It is primarily verbal. It may take the form of a magnificent monologue cataloguing the annoyances, irritants, exasperations and frustrations that have accumulated to the point of explosion over the day, or the week, in the workplace, at home, or in other social contexts.

Venting is deciding that feelings that have been clamped, denied, repressed, suppressed, contained or simply postponed, should be released. It frequently occurs when people have had enough of diplomacy, courtesy, self-restraint, political correctness and self-containment; when people feel it is time to say what 'has to be said', time to release the emotional pressure of keeping one's feelings in check, time to release repressed emotions, to give expression to them in a rant.

Venting is akin to speaking one's mind, laying one's cards on the table, stating the facts, putting the record straight, cutting to the chase, being honest, getting real, saying it 'like it is' and coming clean, even if only to oneself, about how one feels.

Venting is like a psychological expletive, an energising emission, a great grumble, a cerebral carp, a healing whinge, a decisive declaration, a liberating moan. While it may occasionally be an emotional soliloquy, it is more effective if others are present because there is therapeutic power in being listened to with unconditional care.

Some instances of venting mimic curmudgeon-type behaviour: the bah-humbug of people who are overwrought by the inanity of others or by the situations in which they find themselves so that they must tell another person or burst.

In this way venting can be the release of pent-up rage, but it is not necessarily an angry event in the way that anger usually expresses itself. Nor is venting directed, as such, at others. Instead it involves the recruitment of other people as witnesses to one's outburst. It asks others to be observers of one's acknowledgement of the anger, disappointments and frustrations burning within that must find expression and release.

Just as household radiators that are not regularly vented become cold, unresponsive and dysfunctional, so too people who have no emotional outlets lose their happiness, their perspective and their warmth. This is why venting is important.

There is an art to venting. It is not to be undertaken lightly, without knowing that one is venting, and without due consideration of what one hopes to achieve from the vent. The frequency of venting is also important, because to engage too often is to become a grouch, while being afraid to let off steam is to allow unhealthy pressure to build up unnecessarily.

People have personal patterns of venting. It is practiced by some on rare occasions, by others at intervals, while many engage in it with healthy regularity with pre-selected recipients.

This is why the choice of 'ventee' is important. If you are considering choosing someone to vent to, it should be someone whom you trust, someone who knows you well, someone who understands your need to vent occasionally, someone who recognises a good vent when he or she hears it and someone who does not feel obliged to advise but who is prepared to listen to what you have to say.

When recipients are aware that what is occurring is merely venting, that it will rise and subside without the need for any interventions on their part, then venting is invigorating, liberating and useful for everyone. Recipients also often benefit because 'ventors' may be expressing universal annoyances, which makes venting therapeutic to listen to as well as to be heard.

Perhaps this is why many people who vent have reciprocal arrangements with those on whom they vent, through which venting, like peer mentoring, becomes a turn-taking arrangement. Each is prepared to absorb the outburst of the other. Each knows that the other will respond in a caring, confidential way. Practiced well, venting may be safe, therapeutic and cathartic. No harm is done and emotional suppression is avoided.

And when the venting is over, many 'ventors' finalise their verbosity with a smile, a laugh, an apology or a request that they not be taken too seriously, that the content of their vent be ignored and that no response be made, because they were 'only venting'. Most will admit that they feel 'the better' for the vent, that in the process they gained new perspectives and that they are now ready to re-enter the fray. It's good to vent.

–13–

Walking Back To Happiness

'Is there a felicity in the world comparable to this?' asks Marianne in Jane Austen's novel *Sense and Sensibility*, referring to the joys of walking. What a question! What an observation! Because what she recognised then, without the modern parlance on it, is that walking is one of the most enjoyable, most therapeutic, most psychologically interventive of the ordinary activities that we can undertake.

It is freely available. It requires no appointment, no referral letter, no waiting time for consultation. There is no fee. It is a powerful, natural, mood-altering and enhancing exercise. It has anti-depressant ingredients. It is physically beneficial when undertaken sensibly, and it is there at the opening of the hall door any time, day or night. It is a 'felicity' indeed.

Walking helps mental health and well-being, releases tension, stimulates, animates, rejuvenates and invigorates. For those who are finding life to be affirmative, cheerful and satisfying to them, walking is a joyous celebration of that. There is the happy stride, the upbeat gait and the exuberant expression of just how good it is to be alive, mirrored in the secure, sure-footed, confident step, swinging arms and progressive pace of the happy walker.

Walking is especially interventive for those to whom life is being unkind. It entices the person who is feeling low to get up, out of bed, into clothes and out in the fresh air. In so doing it reunites them with the world. But not the world at a manic pace, rather the world at a measured pace, the world at the pace they decide to negotiate it at. It is at the walker's pace. And for that time he or she is in command.

Psychologically the one thing we can measure is our stride when walking. We determine when we go, where we go and how quickly or slowly we get there. When life is overwhelming, when it seems as if nothing is within one's power, when there is a sense of foreboding, of fear, of helplessness, being able to walk is one antidote. It says 'I control me'.

Walking may be around the block, familiarising ourselves with every house and garden, the atmosphere, the sense of place, of where we live

and who lives there, of local dogs and cats, of paved paths and gravelled drives, dishevelled lawns or those meticulously manicured.

Walking can be enjoyed alone or in company, undertaken in silence or with a companion in animated exchange. Walking facilitates inner reflection: the rhythmic movement a physical mantra to soothe the body, to calm the mind and reassure the soul. Problems are solved while walking. Decisions are made. Hurts are released. Joys are celebrated. Perspective is gained. Pain is recognised. Courage restored. All life is with us and we are with ourselves in a unique way while walking.

Walking can begin in beautiful places, by a lake, by the sea, in a forest, across a field, away from urban concreteness with the rugged gentleness of nature. Walking is a calm way to encourage a child, support a young person, solidify a relationship and repair old hurts.

Young people who walk with their parents share something special. Walking allows articulation or silence; it allows questions to be asked, answered or unanswered without the need for eye contact.

Apologies can be given, statements can be made. The act of walking absorbs energy that might otherwise go into heated exchange. There is cooperation in walking, alongside another, going in the same direction, and if the family dog is in tow then who could be angry walking behind a wagging tail?

Metaphorically, walking reminds us that life is about taking it step by step. We decide whether we double back, plough forward against the elements or shelter for a while. We decide who is beside us and how often we stop to appreciate what is close; whether we whizz by or revel in where we are rather than what lies ahead.

Walking has always been the means by which special physical and mental places were sought. For centuries pilgrims progressed across the world, walking staff in hand, hope in heart, with motivation of mind and a willingness to endure whatever was encountered on the road in order to arrive at that person or place that held the answers to the pilgrim's question. Only to find upon arrival that the answer was within themselves all along had they but known. Walking got them there.

It Should Be So Simple

It should be so simple. Life should be easier. With technology removing the burden of many manual and mental tasks, energy should be higher, time should be greater and space should be created for what is important to us.

But this has not happened. It would seem that we are more mentally tired, more physically exhausted, more socially stretched, more work-stressed, more time-tied, with higher expectations of ourselves than ever before. Life has not got easier. It gets harder every day.

With the cutbacks of the recession, those in work find working days are longer, tasks more numerous, time-management more intense, systems more complex and with less personal time, private time, reflective time and family time than ever before.

The maxim that 'all work expands to fill the time available for its execution' suggests that we engage in repetitive, redundant activities to rationalise and occupy our allocated time on tasks, regardless of what time is available to us. But in these tough times we are more likely to do the opposite, to condense time, try to fit more activities into a shorter time than is possible and favour quantity over the quality of what we do.

Each time we invent or invest in a labour-saving commodity, a more rapid means of communication or more diverse communication methods, we can create as many problems as we solve. The propensity to raise the bar is evident. As soon as we find a quicker means of doing something, we either find more of those things to do more quickly or alternative tasks to fill the gap from those previous endeavours.

For example, the original magic of the word processor – its speed, its capacity to alter, insert, delete or expand documents on command, to improve, justify and to print many copies – should surely have reduced the pressure of paperwork in many lives. The converse is true.

If documents are easily typed, then more of them can be prepared. If alterations may be made, then visual perfection is the norm. If copies are available, then everyone should have one. If groups can be contacted,

then everyone should be included, and if replies can go to all, then everyone in the collective receives the reply of everyone else in a way that overloads the mental system and makes the organisation of information excessive and more complex each day.

The capacity to do more should not lead, in a mindless, ill-considered way, to doing more, unless what one is doing is worth doing to begin with and unless it is enhanced by doing more of it.

More is less if life becomes a tyranny of tasks. More is less if we do not create appropriate time to reflect on what we are doing. As individuals and organisations we need to ask, at regular intervals, what are we doing and why? We need to ask if doing more of the same does more for anyone. Recent examples in large organisations of the danger of 'doing' without reflection on the rationale of what is being done has shown how necessary it is to factor self-reflexive practice into our professional lives and our organisational strategies. Size matters. Bigger is not necessarily better. Greater is not necessarily good.

Time matters. If we are accessible all the time then can we be equally mentally available and alert? If there is no reprieve from communication, if there is nowhere that one cannot be contacted, how does that impact on our mental health? We are becoming increasingly clinically aware that if there is no safe zone from phone or text, nowhere we cannot be emailed, faxed and accessed, that this has real psychological stress effects on us in the long term.

The avalanche of emails in the inbox, the number of voicemails that await us overnight, the extent of texts and twitters and the overload of communication means that we cannot truly disconnect from the relentlessness of messages that others wish to send us and to which they want a prompt reply. Divisions between personal time and work time are essential but they are being eroded.

With immediacy of communication there is an expectation of immediate response. Yet if we are to process information properly, reflect upon our answers, consider options, respond in a coordinated way and keep in mind the larger picture in the daily detail, then we need some space to do so. We need recursivity between thinking time and operational time – without which individuals suffer, organisations flounder and things go wrong.

The essential mental rejuvenation and physical regeneration that drawing boundaries between work and home once provided meant that the elastic of working life was stretched often enough to ensure it did not snap. Each of us knows how stretched we are. Scientist Hans Selye's early work in this area on general adaptation syndrome confirms that whether or not we snap under stress depends upon whether there is a regular reprieve from stress, or whether it is persistent and prolonged with no time for ourselves.

Time is our gift. The tyranny of time is our creation. The consequences are clear.

15

Gotta Dash

What a lovely punctuation mark the dash is. How therapeutic it is to focus on it to the exclusion of all other life pressures. When times are tough we need to dash. Dashing is therapeutic because the dash is a sign of hope when it seems that progress has reached a full stop. It is truly a delightful punctuation mark. It is light, entertaining and optimistic – a symbol of good things ahead.

Taking time out to even consider the dash is therapeutic. It is an indulgence that is available and free. For the dash is a positive signal. It is going somewhere – a mark on the move, not something that arrests development of the sentence, but something that elaborates and expands, deviates and delights in one stroke.

The dash carries psychological meaning. Punctuation has its rules, as does life, but dashing defies them and it does so in a swift, sure, stylish manner that is liberating to the mind and the words that flow from it. And the dash is best delivered with a pen – preferably a quill – so that it is executed with a dramatic flourish. Print is fine for hyphens, for their ordered, measured, horizontal exactitude – but the dash is special; it should never be circumscribed. Which is why the lazy dash is an oxymoron – there is nothing lazy about the dash. It energises the writer, allows the free flow of ideas, determines that the next passage is read and flies in the face of pedantic semantic sensibilities.

The dash is an energetic, enthusiastic, enlivening, seductive gigolo that consorts with any sentence, challenges conjunctions, sneers at colons, and resists the curtailment of full stops. It is far superior to the comma, which, with all due respect, slows us down, impedes our progress toward the end of the sentence and has so many rules about when and where it can be used, or must be omitted, that for such a tiny mark it is a hugely tedious modulation. Perhaps this is why writers and dramatists, such as Samuel Beckett and Harold Pinter, and a host of others, ignored it or recruited it to their will; distaining grammatical tyranny in favour of creativity and silences, that no comma could accommodate, nor full stop end.

Granted the comma can be a functional, regulating mark for pitch, tone and rhythm; but it is an inelegant, castrated, tadpole type of thing between clauses – a semantic squiggle that either sprinkles itself too liberally across a paragraph, or it is conspicuous by its absence, as the voice drones on and on unedited and unrestrained until we reach incomprehensibility and yearn for the finality of the full stop.

The comma may be beloved and inspirational for punctuation pedants: editors may argue forever about it, friends may part because of it and meaning may be utterly altered by its absence – but when it comes to the dash, the flippant, debonair dash, little surpasses it, as Emily Dickinson's work can attest.

Take for example the full stop. It is, of course, the most reliable aid to clarity. There, I've said it. You've read it. The sentence is finished. That's it, written, read, understood. That is what makes the full stop definitively depressing.

Unlike the dash – the lively dash, the dash that rushes us to the next proposition – the full stop makes no dangerous punctuation liaisons. It stands alone. It holds no promises for the future. It implies no continuation of the story. It relies on the next sentence for more information. It is curt. It is abrupt. It brooks no argument. It ends our relationship with the sentence in an authoritative way. The sentence is spent. The full stop is the end point of punctuation: done, finished, period. Compared to the dash it is dull.

But wait! Is there some competition for the dash from the exclamation mark? At first glance it might appear to be so, but on inspection there is none. For the exclamation mark is full of self-admiration and conceit. It shrills when it has been amusing, identifying its jokes and explaining them. It is loud, overstated and crude, shouting look at me, me! It lacks the charm and suave sophistication of the dash that entices by its presence rather than pretension.

Yes, the dash does it. And had I more words I would argue its case more cogently, but an editor awaits copy and so I've got to dash!

16

Whole World in a Hug

Do you need a hug? Yes, an old-fashioned, 'come here till I make it better' hug? This is the kind of hug one remembers from childhood. This is the invitation of outstretched arms, the warmth of being enfolded by them, the reassuring squeeze, the closeness, the softness, the safety, the sheer protection and sense of encompassing love that the embrace of a parent provides.

The spontaneous, loving hug is a powerful non-verbal message of closeness and care. It offers a moment away from the maelstrom of life. It gives precious time out. It is an action through which all that exists is gentle, primordial, physical and psychological security. The hug is central to 'attachment' in childhood and adult psychological well-being. We need to hug and be hugged, and clinical wisdom suggests that we neither hug, nor are hugged, enough.

For such a simple act, the hug carries a message of profundity and power. Hugs exceed what can be said. Hugs are simultaneously given and received because you cannot give a hug without getting one, or receive a hug without giving one, making the hug a human act of especial significance and nurturing care.

In childhood hugs epitomise maternal warmth, paternal security and parental nurturance. The hugs of childhood fulfil many primitive psychological functions. They unite and bond. In preverbal parent/child interactions hugs are gentle reminders of affection and protection, kinship and connection, ritual and restorative care. The child who is hugged often, lovingly and gently receives ongoing messages of love and extends that gentleness out towards others in later life. Hugs signal value and worth. Hugs cost nothing but the child denied a hug is impoverished indeed.

Hugs are ways of responding to and repairing the hurts and frights of childhood. They are part of the child's journey towards independence, because the child who is sure of a hug when it is needed is much more assured of its safety when exploring the world around it. It is easier to test the world when there is a safe haven to return to, and one of the nicest

returns from adventure is into parental arms for a 'big hug'. This is a joy that continues throughout life regardless of age, which is why at airports, train stations, bus stations, ports and other points of departure, parents and adult offspring bear-hug each other in order to hold each other emotionally during their time apart.

The need for a hug does not end with childhood. Apart from the romantic hugs of lovers, we continue to value the non-sexual, affectionate, bonding embrace that declares our connections to each other in friendship, common humanity and humanitarian love. Our salutations and farewells, our hugs of sympathy, our hugs of congratulations, our hugs at transitional events, such as weddings and funerals, and on occasions that carry social or psychological significance, all display and transmit the message that hugs are important in personal, social and community life. We need them throughout life, and many adults who feel lonely or alone will describe the emotional aridity of nobody to give them 'a simple hug'.

This may be why so many adults have been known to queue for hours for the warmth of a hug, of pure compassionate love, from the woman known as Amma (meaning 'Mother'). As part of her mission to 'embrace the world', Amma travels the globe with outstretched arms to hold and enfold those who seek the healing power of her perfect hug.

This hug, called 'Darshan', is described as 'a gentle river caressing parched souls'. It is a hug of pure mother love, unity with the ideal mother that perhaps you could not be, or the mother you could not have, or the mother you wished to be, to have, or the mother you have lost. It is described as an awakening, being reunited with oneself while loving humanity. It echoes the Irish adage that 'a mother's love is a blessing', because embraced by Amma's arms, the mind stops, relaxes and learns to love in a nurturing interweave between and towards all people, towards all animals, towards every part of creation.

Regardless of what this says about the psychological complexity of our relationship with idealised motherhood or what sociological interpretation one may place on masses of people demonstrating their adult need for 'mother love' by queuing for a 'mother hug', it is recorded that in excess of 28 million people worldwide have sought and received Amma's hug. This is further recognition that material things do not heal human hurt, loneliness and emotional pain, but genuine acts of love.

17

For Richer, For Poorer, in Recessionary Times

For richer, for poorer, has taken on new significance in many marriages. Recession changes everything. Marriage is no exception. Communicating about finances is something that couples are finding themselves having to do. For many this is difficult. It is a new conversation, and how to conduct it is a challenge, particularly for those who never had to do so before.

There is no doubt that having money can lighten aspects of living and that being without money can strain marriage to a serious extent. But research is also clear that except in situations of absolute impoverishment, it is not necessarily lack of money that destroys a marriage, but rather how couples communicate and negotiate with each other about it that determines how the relationship progresses. It is whether the negotiation is fair, whether or not one person has to sacrifice while the other maintains his or her former financial life, or whether together they both adjust to changes in how they spend.

For many couples, talking about money may be an undeveloped skill, one that they need to acquire quickly, as issues about money, or the lack of money, enters their relationship in a new way. They need to agree that this is something they have to work out. That it is equitable. That it is agreed. That it is worthwhile. That what is most important to them is each other, and that no riches would make up for the loss of the other person in their life.

And they do not just need to communicate with each other. Families with children also have to find creative ways of responding sensitively and realistically to children's demands for goods and activities that the family can no longer afford. Parents need to speak with one voice about this. They need to be together. They need to be sympathetic and clear.

The problem with money is that it can affect so many aspects of life. Having enough money reduces stress in many relationships. Typical examples include the help it can bring with household tasks, saving arguments about who vacuums, dusts or cleans and whether the husband/wife housework ratio is fair. Then there is the psychological relief of coming home at the end of the working day to a clean, tidy, well-ordered space, rather than to the morning's breakfast dishes and last night's dinner plates still in the kitchen sink.

Meals out can take the stress out of a long day. When two working people are tired, neither may have the inclination to cook. Before the recession there was a solution to this. When the fridge was empty, energy was low, irritability was high and hypoglycaemia seemed to be setting in, many couples resolved this by eating out together, to relax, share a glass or two of wine, discuss their working day and generally 'relax, relate, communicate' in each other's company at the end of a long day.

Money bought child-minding. Money bought babysitters. Money bought someone to collect children from school. Money bought time. Money bought stress reducers: sport, hobbies, holidays. Money bought time together and time apart. Money often bought order. Money bought psychological reprieve.

The financial cost of psychological support becomes conspicuous when absent. When money is not available for family tasks, a new way of living is required. Adjusting to recession is not about 'reducing', cutting back, scrimping and saving and shaving off the luxuries of life.

Financial management, from a psychological perspective, is not about adjusting downwards. It is not about taking the hit. It is not about trying to do as much as before with less. Instead, it is about taking on a totally new way of viewing the world. It is about establishing an entirely new way of relating to people, to things, to activities, to objects, to social pressure, to status and to life. It is about different values, different perceptions of what is desirable, different aspirations and different measures of success. Otherwise each day can bring resentment for what is lost rather than revelations about how rewarding life can be, despite having much less money to spend.

Of course an argument such as this can be dismissed as idealistic, unrealistic, inappropriate psychobabble. And for those suffering real and frightening poverty in comparison to the past, of course adjustment is not about perception, it is about getting appropriate financial support. But for many families, the experience of changed financial circumstances, the experience of doing things together, of spending time together, of sharing work, of walking to activities, of returning to self-generated entertainment and increasing self-sufficiency in life has been, by their own accounts, a positive experience.

− 18 −

Life Before Birth

Emotional well-being begins before birth. This is not just because the psychological environment into which a child will be born is significant, but family factors preceding the birth are also important and in their own manner communicate themselves to the baby in utero. They determine the climate in which the pregnancy progresses.

Research provides expanding insights into the postnatal psychological consequences of prenatal life. Life begins not at birth but before it. One piece of evidence for this is the manner in which babies respond to voices, patterns of sounds, melodies and stories that they have heard prenatally when they are exposed to those same sound sequences and experiences after birth.

Babies not only listen and show remarkable discrimination between sounds, but also pay attention to sound patterns and have an extraordinary capacity to distinguish them. Research as far back as the 1980s by DeCasper and Fifer showed that newborns distinguish and prefer their mother's voice from other female voices. Not surprising perhaps, given that this voice is dominant prenatally. But what is perhaps more interesting is the experiment in which pregnant women read a particular story repeatedly in the final six weeks of pregnancy to their unborn babies. After birth, it was evident that the newborn responded more to the story they heard in their final six weeks' gestation than to new stories heard after their birth.

This shows that even before birth infants are paying attention to and discriminating amongst measurable complex sound configurations. The baby in the womb is attuned to the world outside it.

The implications of this are considerable in emotional terms. They tell us that the baby is 'listening' to the world he or she will enter. Babies hear the world before they join it. They are learning about it before they are born. This accounts for how much babies love to vocalise, how infants love rhyme, how children learn from rhythm and rhyme and the emotional repertoire to which music exposes us throughout life.

Hearing is the last sense to leave us as we leave the world. It would seem to be equally significant before we enter it.

The capacity to be attuned to melody, to appreciate the cadences of poetry, to listen to the tone of a story, to become accustomed to language – these potentials are not just laid down in a genetic code but seem to be enhanced by the opportunities provided before birth.

If we follow this line of thinking to a logical conclusion, then there is also the converse: that the baby may be disadvantaged before birth if its parents are in a poor relationship, if there are harsh words, angry exchanges, raised voices and particularly if there are episodes of violence. Knowing the attention paid by the yet-to-be-born baby to what is happening in the personal world he or she will enter warns us about many things.

It reminds us that exposure to a harsh auditory world is something a child might need protection from before birth and not just after it, and that a safe, secure, calm, prenatal world has implications for psychological life.

The negative consequences of smoking, alcohol intake, poor diet and adverse physical environments are well documented. But while the many isolated strands of research about the prenatal capacities of the baby are known, specific guidelines with regard to emotional protection have been less clear about how to support mothers in an extra special way during their pregnancies.

Inevitably, some of the research on womb life has been exploited in educational programmes by those who promote prenatal education for intellectual advancement and advantage over others. But that is not the primary purpose of research on intrauterine conditions. Rather than exploiting knowledge about life in the womb for competitive gain, this is information to be used to provide the most conducive environment for the development of human potential, happiness, security and love in order to lay down the psychological foundation that will support the child through all the developmental stages that lie ahead.

Of course mothers do not need research to tell them about the active communicative bond between them and their babies. They talk to them. Many instinctively know the music their babies like. They know and note their periods of activity and quiescence. They reassure them. They know their babies before they meet them. And their babies know them.

Childhood

Childhood is a short eternity. Its years are few, but its influence is forever. Its memories last a lifetime. Moments can be remembered as hours; hours as weeks; weeks as years; and intense events as if they were without end. What is experienced in childhood is etched in the conscious or unconscious mind for the rest of a person's life.

Childhood shapes the mind. Childhood shapes imagination. Childhood shapes the capacity to engage with others, the ability to trust people, the skill to communicate with them, a person's sense of self, of acceptance, of power, of place in the world, of identity and of life itself.

Childhood memories are vivid. They are visceral. They have a depth, strength and a power that is greater than at other times in life. Living is intense. Nothing escapes the eye of the child. Objects appear and disappear. Patterns are vibrant. Lights are bright. Darkness is black. Sensory experiences glide into each other. Memories are eidetic. Images are engraved on memory forever.

Nothing escapes the ears of a child. Ears are always listening and open. More than words are heard. Meaning is attached. Speed rhythm and pitch of conversation are interpreted. Tone is absorbed. Body language is noted. Silences are heard. Silences are understood.

Fragrances are important in childhood: the smell of fresh sheets, of new shoes, of winter clothes, of summertime, of animals, of people, of perfume, of alcohol or tobacco on adults, of the sea, of grass, of food and cooking, the smell of the streets, of home and of the world.

The child's world is tactile. Everything is felt. Human touch is gentle or harsh, reassuring or frightening, careless, careful or neglectful, present or absent, impatient, callous or kind. The feel of fabric is important. Clothes are coarse or soft, warm or cool, heavy or light, ugly or beautiful. Objects are of noticeable texture, weight, size and dimension.

The child's world is often circumscribed by distance from home and sense of place: the house, the garden, the local roads, the nearest town, the community hall, the church, the shops, the mall. Living is in the detail.

It remembers each step on the way to and from school, the smell of the classroom, the sight of the person who sits in front, beside or behind. There is the light from high windows, the voice of the teacher, the rummage in bags, the rustle of books, the routine and rhythm and chants of class, the sounds of the playground, the beginning and end of the day.

Childhood is chronologically determined and physically bounded. Its years are not many but they are crucial ones. And a child who suffers in childhood carries that pain for a long, long time. This is why childhood deserves protection, immediate intervention if it goes wrong, preferential treatment, and rights that are not dependent upon the whim of adults, the vigilance of neighbours, the courage of strangers or the efficiency of services. The needs and rights of the child should be unassailable, inalienable, identified and implemented on time.

If the view of the child is not understood, is it because questions are not asked of those who know about children or not asked of children themselves about what they need? If questions are asked and the answers are not responded to, then why are children let down? If we know what children need, then why is it not provided? If we care about children, then why are children not put first, in protection, in policy and its enactment?

When a child suffers, society is damaged. The suffering of children hurts us all. It raises questions about what kind of people we are that can allow children to endure poverty, neglect, hardship and distress as so many do. It says that our past is not past but present and that the child in Ireland remains relatively inaudible in the adult world.

Each new situation that emerges about children suffering provides one more example of where children stand in the hierarchy of power. Not strong. Not high. Not large. They are small, fragile and dependent. Children have no vote. The rights of adults have almost always overridden the rights of the child in our culture despite the hyperbolic, aspirational rhetoric surrounding the establishment of the State and declarations of care for children since then.

It is time for us to reflect again on how we care for childhood, remembering that a year is little in a lifetime, but it is a lifetime in the life of a child.

– 20 –

Colouring In

When parents look for occupations to engage young children during the holidays, few pastimes can compete with colouring. Yes, paper and crayons, coloured pencils, felt tips or Magic Markers for colouring provide entertainment and developmental opportunities for children.

Colouring is a portable occupation, time-consuming, creative and imaginative, while also facilitating emotional expression and artistic development in one simple activity.

Colouring employs a range of skills. It develops visual and spatial awareness. Colouring an outlined picture and choosing and confining the colours within the demarcated lines allows additional fine-tuning of motor abilities and helps a child to calibrate physical movement and negotiate hand-eye coordination in a special, educative and enjoyable way. Looking through 'colouring books' one can trace a child's developing confidence and increased skill when more colours remain 'inside the lines' than outside them.

The most obvious learning through colouring is learning the names of colours and experiencing the colours as they are named, which is both a visual and an emotional experience as the beauty of colour is absorbed by a child. Creating the colour on the page is an activity that alerts the mind to colour through two senses, vision and touch, and this makes colours become even more alive in a child's mind.

While most children know the primary colours, not all have access to the full spectrum of colour, and attuning children to shades of colour develops their descriptive vocabulary in relation to colour and appreciation of colour nuances for later life.

But more is learnt when colouring than just the names of colours. Crayons and pencils can be counted before and after colouring, extending the learning into numeracy. Pencils may be returned to their containers in order, tidied and sharpened for the next time they are required. Minding objects, appreciating them, placing a value on them

and recognising the benefits of caring for one's possessions are also valuable learning experiences for children.

Colouring can be free range, with rainbows of colours and kaleidoscopes of graduated shades adorning the page. There is satisfaction, imagination and liberation in using whatever colour attracts, and watching as it reveals itself as directed by a tiny hand and a thinking mind.

Sometimes, inadvertently, overlays of colour expose the colour spectrum and how it is composed, as combinations merge to provide other colours. This is revelation. This is magic. This is scientific experiment in action. This is the child exploring aspects of the world and discovering that in every action there is a reaction; that he or she can be causative in creation.

Watching how children colour gives insight into their perception of the world. Are colours portrayed as found in nature? Is the grass green? Is the sky blue, the sun yellow? Or is 'reality' challenged, is reality what the child decides that it is, wishes it to be and so creates it?

What about free drawing? What about family portraits? How are family members portrayed and proportioned. Are they aligned neatly or scattered across the page. Are they juxtaposed according to their relationships with each other, their liking for each other, their communication with each other and their wish to be 'drawn' together?

Are emotional closeness and distance represented by where family members are put? Are those who are drawn in large scale emotionally large in the child's life? Are those whom they do not like minimised, omitted or consigned to the farthest corner of the page? Who is smiling? Who is laughing? Whose eyes are open, whose eyes are closed? Who is playing and who is standing still?

Drawing is an activity for indoors on a rainy day or outside when the sun is shining. Encouraging children to draw what they see when they are in the garden, or on an outing, when they are at the sea, or in the park, or looking at animals or plants, enhances observation, perception and appreciation of the world in which they live.

Fingers and Toes

One of the first acts by new parents immediately after the birth of their baby is to count the baby's fingers and toes. Many parents give accounts of doing so: quickly, silently, fearfully and automatically to establish that all is well.

Counting provides objective, numeric assurance that what should be there is there: eyes, ears, nose, mouth, fingers and toes. If all are present in the right order and number, parents usually feel reassured that their baby will not be challenged by difference in life. That is the wish of each parent.

At birth, gender is verified, the child is held, the face is examined, the eyes are sought and the automatic quick counting of fingers and toes is completed. But the preoccupation with fingers and toes does not end there, because fingers and toes continue to play a role in the emotional and educational life of the child. And of course in later life, even in these somewhat cynical times about relationships, it is still custom to place a specific ring upon a particular finger to seal the deal of lifelong partnership.

Fingers and toes serve as inbuilt calculators. The first counting games are played with children using their fingers and toes. Most children will have experienced the terrifying delight of the toe pulling involved in the rhyme about the piggies going to the market. In that traditional game each toe is pulled in turn. The first represents the 'little piggy' that went to the market; the second toe the piggy that stayed at home; while the third got bread and butter and the fourth had none. Then comes the culmination of this childhood ritual as the little toe is caught in a dramatic hold to the refrain 'and this little piggy went whee, whee, whee all the way home'.

Fingers are the best toys. They are available at all times. When travelling with children they are priceless. They can be examined, used to tap out rhythm and time, be intertwined. They are the source of endless games, counting rhymes and songs. They make animal shapes, which in addition to learning about nature, fires the imagination through symbolic play. They are the immediate distraction for the fractious child, particularly

if ritualistic songs have already been established using them, because children love ritual, love to know what is going to happen next, love the inbuilt repetition of their favourite games.

Fingers are invaluable when no other toys are available. They are the 'legs' of 'incy, wincy spider' climbing up the child's arm to tickle under the chin. They are the hands and feet of the fine lady with 'rings on her fingers and bells on her toes'. They are imaginative opposing armies of five against five.

Toes have the added advantage that fingers can manipulate them and so expand play in creative ways. When children are learning to count, using both their fingers and toes extends numeric options to twenty. In school, addition and subtraction are visible as fingers are held up or folded down, providing two learning modalities in one: the chanting of numbers and the accompanying actions of the fingers when doing so.

During the pre-language stage, infants point to the object he or she requires. And language is acquired as parents automatically name all that the child identifies by that tiny digit making the request. Children enjoy sharing a book of familiar pictures, pointing as parents ask them to identify each one. Sign language provides children with hearing impairments with an important means of connecting with the world, and fingers flying in this communication are impressive to watch.

The emotional function of fingers is not to be dismissed. Fingers assist the expression of feelings when they are bunched, aimed, twisted, hidden or opened with delight. In anger they may be used to pinch or prod another child or to gesture insults at them; while all children know what an adult means when a finger is pointed or wagged at them.

Fingers stretch out to grasp life. Most parents remember the first time their own index finger was clutched by the tiny grasping fist of their newborn child, the first time a hand reached out for theirs and those fingers walked o'er their hearts 'with gentle gait' and lifelong bond.

−22−

Spontaneity May Be Required

Parenting has become too prescriptive. There are too many contradictory rules. Some say that it has become professionalised and circumscribed, task oriented, goal directed, and that many parents feel disempowered by this. That is why 'spontaneity' may be a liberating parenting approach for both parent and child.

Children who are joyous, energetic and spontaneous gather friends around them. They send out positive messages to others and receive positive affirmations in return. They are more likely to be the first who are chosen for teams, the people others want to befriend and the kind of people their classmates would like to be. They are active, effervescent, willing to explore, to try new games, to welcome the new pupil into the school, to sign up for sporting and creative activities and to have a positive approach to life.

Children who are spontaneous reach out rather than close up in response to novelty. They are often described as daring, happy-go-lucky and adventurous. People tend to be positive about them, which, with classic Pygmalion effect, charms their lives. Their confidence is high and their self-esteem is good because they have a collection of evidential experiences of competence to reassure them about their capabilities when the next challenge appears.

Whether or not children are gifted with spontaneity depends on many factors: family history, parental optimism and extended family relationships at the time the child was born. It may depend upon the temperament of the child, early life experiences, position in family, disposition of siblings and the models of behaviour available from significant others around the child. In the family that is overly cautious, pessimistic, risk-aversive, wary – of spontaneous behaviour and fearful of spur-of-the-moment activities, spontaneity, as a way of responding to life, is unlikely to develop. That is why amongst all the wonderful ideas with which parents may imbue their children, helping children to be spontaneous is important because it equips them to respond to life and to live responsively.

Spontaneous play between parent and child is a feature of parent–child interactions. Turn taking, peek-a-boo, imitative behaviour and improvisation are all part of play. What makes play different to goal-directed behaviour is that it is liberating, it is imaginative, it is intuitive, it is without constraint and it is not concerned with outcomes but with living in the moment. The process of play is its most important component.

In psychotherapy with children, improvisation, spontaneity and responsiveness are intrinsic to the psychotherapeutic process. Following where the child leads, entering imaginatively into the child's world or the world the child creates for the therapist, participating in the lives of fictional characters created by the child and listening to the child's spontaneous stories are essential ingredients in therapy.

Children who are helped to be spontaneous have been given a special approach to life. For spontaneity is a gift. It is the art of the impromptu. It is knowing how to say yes to the unexpected: responding to the spur-of-the-moment opportunity, seizing all that is given and not having to deliberate obsessively before embarking on potential adventures offered in life. To be spontaneous is to be courageous, optimistic and intuitive, to believe that saying yes will bring more rewards than will saying no and opting out. It is seeing the potential in every situation and recognising its possibilities.

Adults who are responsibly spontaneous provide a model of life for their children. They show that spontaneity is about savouring the moment, making the most of what is available. Spontaneity is a form of optimism but it exceeds optimism because it actually acts upon that positive ideology in everyday life.

Spontaneity invites friends home without worrying what is in the fridge. Spontaneity responds to last-minute tickets at the theatre. Spontaneity celebrates all achievements. It accepts all invitations and lives life to the full.

Spontaneity is what energises us about jazz, what we appreciate in tap-dancing and what we love most about the unplanned sign-song that brings joy to all who join in. Spontaneity is sweeping your child up for a dance, bursting into song, and occasionally providing an unexpected treat for no other reason than because life itself is always worth celebrating.

Children who watch their parents behave in joyous, spontaneous but responsible ways find life exciting, the world secure and the future full of possibilities. They respond to opportunities, enjoy challenges and avail of lucky breaks.

Teaching children to be spontaneous in responsible ways is not teaching them to be irresponsible, incautious, rash or impetuous. It is not about impulsive or risky behaviour. It is not inappropriate abandonment of required duties and obligations. But it is a message that life is to be celebrated, it is to be lived, worked at and responded to, and that if you meet it half-way it will be a more joyous journey for you and for others.

23

Talk When It's Tough

Conversations between parents and young people are often distinguished by their brevity. They can end before they have begun. They may consist of a few predictable sentence exchanges. These may foreclose conversation. Alternatively conversations may become contentious unnecessarily. And the sad thing about poor communication is that the worse it gets, the worse it gets: it does not get better when it is bad.

If a pattern of communication that is frustrating to everyone has arisen, then a new pattern is required. This means new questions, new ways of asking them, new contexts in which they are asked, a different tone of voice when asking them or a new receptiveness to answers given.

The timing of conversations is important: there is time to listen to what the young person has to say. And listening is the key to parent–child conversations. Because if we believe we know the answers before we have heard them, then the questions are perfunctory, communication is thwarted and conversation in the sense of meaningful exchange is over before it has begun.

Central to developing new, more positive patterns of communication, is that the questions asked are not closed questions: that they are not questions to which there is only a 'yes' or 'no' answer, because questions requiring a 'yes' or 'no' answer or a single-word response can be experienced as intrusive or disinterested. The problem with closed questions is that they receive closed answers. They do not invite elaboration unless the respondent wishes to provide it. And while the questions may be well-intentioned, they do not encourage discussions in which young people may feel comfortable speaking about what is important to them.

Of course, the classic closed questions are those that adults direct at children whom they do not know well. *What age are you? What class are you in? What school do you go to? What do you want to be when you grow up?* If ever there were conversation stoppers, this series of questions serve that purpose, which is why children provide polite answers knowing that the

questioner is not comfortable in their presence. When an adult reaches for the safety of closed, factual questions, the child knows more about the adult than the adult has learnt about the child!

In a different way, conversations between parents and teenagers also often take a predictably pedantic course because the questions asked prohibit discussion. Think of the difference between being asked 'are you okay?' (fine) or 'what's wrong?' (nothing) or even worse 'what's wrong with you?' (exit teenager).

Invitations to conversation are important to young people. Even when invitations are not immediately accepted they are always appreciated. Knowing that when they want to talk, there is a parent who is ready to listen, is enormously reassuring. Knowing that their feelings have been noticed, even if offers to talk about them are initially rejected, often means that the young person will talk about those feelings later when they are ready to do so. Even if they do not feel ready, they at least know that there is observation and concern being expressed and that they can go to their parents when the time is right.

As in any relationship, conversations between parents and teenagers are not singular events. The do not take place in a vacuum. They occur in the context of parent–teenager relationships: in their capacity to talk to and listen to each other and their determination to find a way to do so.

Paradoxically, the key to 'talking to teenagers' is not to talk but to listen. It is to listen without interruption. It is to listen attentively. It is to listen and allow a silence without filling it with solutions, because from that silence, if the silence is tolerated instead of being filled with remedies, the young person may find the courage to say more.

It is always helpful to wait for more to be said. If necessary some prompts may be given; for example: *Say more about that so that I can understand it more. What is the meaning of that for you?*

It is often useful to communicate your wish to understand more. *If I understood how you are feeling now, what would I know? Can you help me to understand more about this?*

If accused of not caring, not understanding or not listening, that too can be clarified; for example: *If I understood this better, if I was responding the way you would wish me to, what would I be doing? What would I be saying?*

Only towards the end of a conversation should solutions be discussed *What do you think the solution is? Who can help with that?*

Conversations occur when time is spent talking rather than dispensing parental advice. Positive conversations are dependant on the reason the conversation is begun. Any conversation begun in good faith, with love and in an attempt to truly hear and understand the perspective of another person (which does not necessarily mean agreement with it) cannot go too far off track.

Young people need to have positive conversations with their parents. They need opportunities to express what they think, say how they feel, discuss their ideas and articulate their concerns. They need to describe their hopes, tell their fears, share their achievements, explain their worries. They need to talk to someone when things go right, when they are happy, when things go wrong, when they are hurt, when they are confident about life and when they are trying to make sense of their world.

If parent–child communication has been poor, then the next conversation needs to be about communication itself. And what better question to begin that conversation with than *Do you think that I listen to you enough when we talk?*

Talking about talking is often the way to begin talking. Because to talk about how we talk, when we talk, how we listen, when to ask questions and when to be silent, is a new conversation that rarely goes wrong.

As times get tougher and life seems to be more difficult for everyone, the simple acts of talking and listening are free and life-enhancing for everyone.

24

Autumn – The Best of Seasons

To everything there is a season and the season to live it up is autumn. Traditional metaphor for the older years of life, autumn has always been the best season. It has none of the fanfare and busybodyiness of spring with its startling green, its razzmatazz, its 'look at me, I've arrived', its exaggerated promises. Autumn is itself and it is wonderful.

Autumn has none of the clammy cloyness of summer, all dressed up and stressed out by how soon it will end, trying to pack in every moment in the searing sun, or having to swallow disappointment when the season that should be brightest is overcast. Summer has expectations of itself that autumn does not have. Autumn knows itself.

Autumn gives no false promises. It has no fanfare. It is quietly confident. It does not hop, get in a strop or shout. It has learned that understatement is better than exaggeration. It accepts the bad press that it gets. Autumn understands the distortion, the misrepresentation, the inequality of its position, the ignorance of its beauty, the assumptions of its status and the disregard for its worth. It is secure in the secret knowledge of itself that is not available to those who have not yet reached that season.

Those who know autumn know how great it is, when, to quote Albert Camus, 'every leaf is a flower'. Think of the abundance of that. Think of the beauty of that. Autumn is another time in our lives to have fun and the capacity to do so is high. That is autumn's imperative: that it not be wasted but be appreciated and every second of its time used well.

Keats rightly brought recognition to autumn as mellow, mature, ripe and sweet. Autumn has it all, and so should we when we reach that stage in our lives. It is our season. It is the time that is 'loaded and blessed', when all is ripeness to the core. It is time to 'swell the gourd', cherish the secret variegated vibrancy of autumn's colours, the verve, the vivacity, life being lived.

Autumn is not competitive. It allows the preceding seasons to be. It supports them. It is secure in itself. It is in no hurry. It waits until they are

done with rushing and ripening, being busy and budding. Then autumn gathers all that richness, savours its abundance and sizzles silently in its own quiet way. Autumn is wise.

Autumn is a time when we relish who we are, when we appreciate each moment of each day, the presence of others whom we love and the many friends in our lives.

There are axioms that make the experience of autumn most fulfilling: looking back in understanding, not in anger; allowing others who are embroiled in earlier seasons to live their own lives; identifying all that is positive in the autumn season and planning ahead carefully and well.

Autumn allows the best of all worlds: to be indoors by a fire or outdoors in the rich crispness of its days. It allows travel with greater ease than in crowded summer months, or staying at home to learn about all around us. Autumn is about identifying what is genuine in life and then living life authentically. Autumn is real.

Autumn brings freedom because it is without conceit; without concern about the views of others, except those who warrant respect. Autumn is without regrets that are destructive. It is without fear for the future because there is still time to do whatever needs to be done. It should be without worry about the present because so much has already been survived.

In autumn, life can be lived to the fullest by recognising the years behind, the experiences gained, the knowledge acquired and the wisdom accrued. Autumn is the season of gratitude.

You don't waste time when you have reached a half century or more, because it is time to look ahead to the next half century and live it up to the full.

— 25 —

Something To Look Forward To

It is important to have something to look forward to. It is important mental health strategy: to know that there is something positive that is definitely going to happen. It does not have to be something momentous. It may be looking forward to a time in the day, to acquiring a desired object, attending an event, enjoying a fancy food, spending a few precious minutes alone or having time in the company of someone special. However small, however trivial or inconsequential the anticipated time, object or event may be, it is important in psychological terms to have it to look forward to, because having something to look forward to is an important antidote to depression.

Anticipating some future occurrence, no matter how significant or small, is a simple psychological interruption in the pattern of distress and it is one that is much more easily exercised and far more immediately effective than people may think. It is also a useful concept for parents to teach their children about life.

Knowing that something good is going to happen tomorrow helps many people get through today. The child who has nothing to look forward to is truly miserable. If school brings no happiness, if home brings no reprieve, if friends are unattainable, if happy future events are unimaginable and if having something to look forward to is unachievable, then there is little joy in life. This is a dangerous emotional place for anyone to inhabit. It needs to be altered by anticipating something good occurring in the future. We look to the horizon for hope. The emotional horizon must contain promise or else we despair.

Just as something so light, so seemingly immaterial as a straw can become 'the last straw', the psychological breaking point, so too can tiny, apparently trivial occurrences lift people out of gloom and make them feel happy again. For example, young people who are promised a shopping spree when their self-esteem is low may be heartened immeasurably by that. Unexpected treats remind them that life holds unforeseen gifts. Adolescents who are suddenly offered a lift to meet their friends, who

are collected out of the blue when the weather turns bad, who have their favourite meal prepared for them, or who are occasionally slipped some unexpected euro, will feel cheered by the interest shown in them and in their lives.

Even seemingly small acts of care can make a major difference when someone young is feeling down. Showing an interest, displaying concern, communicating support and providing things to look forward to, however small these may be, are genuine therapeutic interventions for depression.

In terms of mental health, it is good to keep organising things to look forward to. Those who plan ahead in this way have been found to be less prone to stress and thereby more resistant to depression. They know what nice things lie in wait. Of course, what constitutes 'something to look forward to' is as diverse as individuals. For some it is being with people. For others it is time alone. Some savour the thought all day of specific evening entertainment: a TV programme, a film, meeting a friend, or a walk around the block with the dog. For some, these small daily inducements keep life on an even emotional keel. Others prefer to plan more major future events, which is why booking the annual holiday is so important for many people.

Book lovers often get through life emotionally by always having some piece of literature to hand. They cannot wait to return to the joy of the text and the unfolding of the story from which they had to extricate themselves. Author G.K. Chesterton once said, 'Just the knowledge that a good book is awaiting one at the end of a long day makes that day happier', and nobody who is immersed in a novel would disagree with him on that.

For many people music is their balm: each familiar note changes their heartbeat, alters their respiration and energises them in a special way. They know that once the music surges through them, their cares will disappear. Some people love to rush up mountains, walk by the sea or be anywhere that is away from urban life. Others like the bright lights of the urban setting, the noise and hubbub of the city.

Stories of concentration camp survivors often refer to the tiniest of objects, activities or beliefs that sustained them. They recall how a piece of string, held close and hidden, became personal and precious; something to use imaginatively or practically, something to look forward to, which was psychologically sufficient to surmount the most inconceivable suffering in life.

If we wish to help people emotionally and to give them hope, then reminding them that they are important, providing something to reassure them and something to look forward to are simple ways of bringing that help and hope. So simple that we often forget that it is not major therapeutic strategies that are required when life seems grim but the simple strings of hope that are to be found in something to look forward to.

No Matter What Pours Down On Us, We Can Survive

How beautiful is the rain!' exclaimed the poet Longfellow, a sentiment not always shared until we reflect upon it and realise how beautiful rain is indeed.

Conspicuous by its absence, rather than appreciated for its presence, rain is an essential psychological presence in our lives; to be Irish is to have an intimate, linguistic, sensory, social and psychological relationship with rain.

Commentary on the weather provides social cohesion. It is salutation and conversation, and anyone stuck for words of greeting, passing comment, or topic for discussion has a ready subject in Irish weather and the likelihood or otherwise of rain.

But rain provides more than ease of social exchange. It is woven linguistically into our lives. It has its own vocabulary and turn of phrase. When it is especially prolific and beautiful, the 'heavens open'. When it is sudden and pours down mercilessly, it 'buckets', it 'rains cats and dogs', and we are treated to 'right' downpours. Sometimes it lingers or falls so lightly that it is almost imperceptible, bringing a 'soft day' through which light is diffused, nature is quiescent and we are psychologically soothed by its sizzling presence in our lives.

Sometimes rain is joyous. Symphonic. Onomatopoeic. It splishes and splashes, plips and plops, splatters and clatters, pitters and patters, tracks and trickles. It beats against doors to get in. It makes rivulets by roadsides. It gathers in gulleys. It drums. It pounds upon windscreens. It colludes with the wind screeching and swirling, swishing and scratching, pouring and pounding. It rushes and gushes. It sends us scuttling for shelter in doorways, under newspapers, grabbing fragments of clothing for protection against its sudden onslaught and the ferocity of its force.

Rain provides emotional expression when its 'tears' trickle down windowpanes for poets. 'Blessed are the dead that the rain rains upon' wrote Edward Thomas, perhaps because a bright day feels too garish for a funeral, too gaudy for our sorrow, or because nature raining in sympathy assures us that it notes our loss.

Rain has its own attire: hats and caps, brollies and macs, the hood, the sou'wester, wellies and galoshes. But while adults wear rainwear for protection, children appreciate the entertainment rain provides: puddles to peer in, to jump in, water to splash, watching it spray upwards into the light. Oh the power of a puddle, the primitive happiness of seeing its smooth surface, running into it, dispersing it, and the joy of squelching boots, drenched socks and mud spattered everywhere.

It is good for children to listen to nature, to listen to the rain, to identify its moods, to name and describe rain's sounds and to attend to them.

It is good for us too in these times of stress to attune ourselves to what is cleansing and refreshing, invigorating and restorative in nature, to turn off the relentless media rhetoric of economic despair and enjoy what is free and familiar and abundant in our lives. There is joy in standing by a window watching the rain do its worst from the protection of indoors. There is equal liberation in abandonment to the elements, in the freedom of going out well wrapped and waterproofed to walk in and enjoy the rain.

Reconnecting with nature is therapeutic. It awaits us. It imposes no charges. It carries no cost. It is not taxed. It is always available and always free. It requires only our presence and respect. Nature reminds us of what we had before boom and bust, of what will be there when this time is over and long after we have gone. It reminds us that whatever we have lost or gained, been given or had taken away, nature remains, steadfast, real and ready to embrace us.

Acknowledgements

I am most grateful to *The Irish Times* for the privilege of writing in its pages, to its editor Geraldine Kennedy, HEALTHplus editor Deirdre Veldon and the generosity and warmth of all my colleagues there. It was a joy to be commissioned to the original team of 'Health Supplement' clinical writers with fellow psychologist Dr Tony Bates and with the late Mr Maurice Neligan, whose presence from its pages will always be missed. Without *The Irish Times*, this book would not exist.

I appreciate the opportunity that was afforded by the *Mindtime* Psychology Series on RTÉ Radio One's *Drivetime*, which was initiated by its former series producer Marian Richardson and supported by the professionalism of presenter Mary Wilson. Thank you Marian and Mary for that wonderful broadcasting year.

As I leave University College Dublin to take up new professional opportunities, this book provides me with an occasion to thank many academic friends there, the student support service staff, and most especially the students in UCD, whose future careers I will follow with interest and pride.

May I also acknowledge friends and colleagues in the Psychological Society of Ireland, the Family Therapy Association of Ireland, the European Association of Psychotherapy, the Tavistock and Portman Clinic London and fellow members of the Medical Council of Ireland.

I have been the beneficiary of the professionalism of the wonderful team in Veritas and would like to thank Managing Director Maura Hyland and Commissioning Editor Donna Doherty, who asked me to consider this collection, and Manager of Publications Caitriona Clarke for her expertise.

As ever there is no meaning to anything that does not have the love and support of family. Thank you a thousand times.